INSPIRATIONAL LIVES

BRADLEY WIGGINS

CHAMPION CYCLIST

Clive Gifford

WAYLAND

First published in 2013 by Wayland

Copyright © Wayland 2013

Wayland
338 Euston Road
London NW1 3BH

Wayland Australia
Level 17/207 Kent Street
Sydney, NSW 2000

Editor: Nicola Edwards
Design: Basement68

British Library cataloguing
in Publication Data
Gifford, Clive.
Bradley Wiggins. -- (Inspirational lives)
  1. Wiggins, Bradley, 1980- --Juvenile
literature.
  2. Cyclists--Great Britain--Biography-
-Juvenile literature. 3. Bicycle racing--
Juvenile literature.
  I. Title II. Series
  796.6'2'092-dc23

ISBN: 978 0 7502 7737 2

Printed in China

Wayland is a division of
Hachette Children's Books,
an Hachette UK company.

www.hachette.co.uk

Picture acknowledgements:
The author and publisher would like
to thank the following for allowing
their pictures to be reproduced in this
publication: Cover Getty Images; p4 PA
Wire; p5 Alex Livesey/Getty Images; p6
John Giles/PA Wire/Press Association
Images; p7 Ben Birchall/LOCOG/Press
Association Images; p8 David Cannon/
Getty Images; p9 Getty Images For TFL;
p10 Toby Melville/PA Archive/Press
Association Images; p11 Jamie McDonald/
ALLSPORT; p12 Tom Hevezi/PA Archive/
Press Association Images; p13 John Giles/
PA Wire; p14 Alexander Hassenstein/
Bongarts/Getty Images; p15 John Giles/
PA Wire; p16 FRANCK FIFE/AFP/Getty
Images; p17 Jasper Juinen/Getty Images;
p18 Bryn Lennon/Getty Images; p19
AP Photo/Christophe Ena; p20 Radu
Razvan / Shutterstock.com; p21 PA Wire;
p22 Pete Goding/Press Association
Images; p23 Laurent Cipriani/AP/Press
Association Images; p24 AP Photo/
Christophe Ena; p25 Pete Goding/Press
Association Images; p26 JOEL SAGET/AFP/
GettyImages; p27 Lewis Whyld/PA Wire;
p28 Getty Images; p29 Anthony Devlin/PA

Contents

Golden summer   4

Growing up   6

Starting cycling   8

A first taste of glory   10

Highs and lows   12

Olympic dreams   14

T king on The Tour   16

Part of a team   18

A defining season   20

Le Gentleman   22

A day in the life of Bradley Wiggins   24

Away from competition   26

The impact of Bradley Wiggins   28

H ve you got what it takes to
be a cycling champion?   30

Glossary   31

Index   32

Golden summer

August 1st, 2012 and the London Olympics men's **time trial** was under way. Every 90 seconds another rider began the 44km-long course, aiming to finish it in the fastest possible time. Tens of thousands of people, many waving 'Wiggo' flags or wearing stick-on sideburns in tribute to Bradley Wiggins' hairstyle, lined the course, hoping to catch a glimpse of the British cyclist as he sped past. Bradley was the last rider to go.

Just four days earlier, he had ridden his heart out in the Olympic road race in an unsuccessful attempt to get his teammate Mark Cavendish into a winning position.

A week before that, Bradley had become the first British rider to win the greatest cycle race in the world – the *Tour de France* – an astonishing achievement.

Bradley, in the race leader's yellow jersey, rides at the front of the peleton during the 2012 Tour de France.

INSPIRATION

After the race, Bradley explained how the sport can inspire others. "The great thing about cycling is that this facility here didn't cost anything to build. So when this is all over anybody can go ride that circuit and pretend they're one of us. That's the great thing with cycling, anybody can do it."

Despite having put his body through these immense strains just days earlier, Wiggins was favourite to win the time trial and add to his haul of Olympic medals. The race was not a foregone conclusion, though. The other 36 riders competing in the time trial were high class and included the 2008 Olympic champion, Fabian Cancellara, and the current world champion, Tony Martin.

At the first time check, less than 10km into the race, tension ran through the crowd at the news that Wiggins was five seconds down on the **pacesetter**, Tony Martin. But they needn't have worried. In an event often decided by single seconds or fractions of a second, Bradley's slick, smooth riding style tore through the field. His winning time of 50 minutes, 39.54 seconds was 42 seconds faster than silver medallist Tony Martin and 68 seconds faster than fellow GB teammate, Chris Froome who won bronze. The giant crowd were elated at Team GB's second gold medal of the Games.

TOP TIP

Bradley never forgets to thank those who've supported him throughout his cycling career. Straight after winning the Olympic time trial, he cycled back down part of the course, giving fans a chance to see and cheer him.

Day five of the 2012 London Olympics and Bradley poses for a photo with a Union Jack flag and his Olympic gold medal around his neck. Wiggins also rang the bell to mark the start of the Olympics opening ceremony.

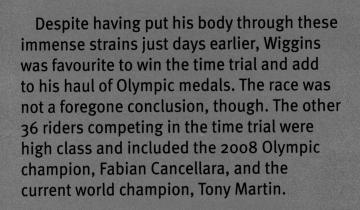

Growing up

Bradley Marc Wiggins was born on April 28th 1980 in the Belgian town of Ghent. His father, Garry, was an Australian racing cyclist who competed in tough road races in Europe. Garry had met Bradley's mother, Linda, in London in 1976 and the couple had married in 1979, but the marriage was short-lived and Garry abandoned his family in 1982. Bradley wouldn't see his father again for 17 years.

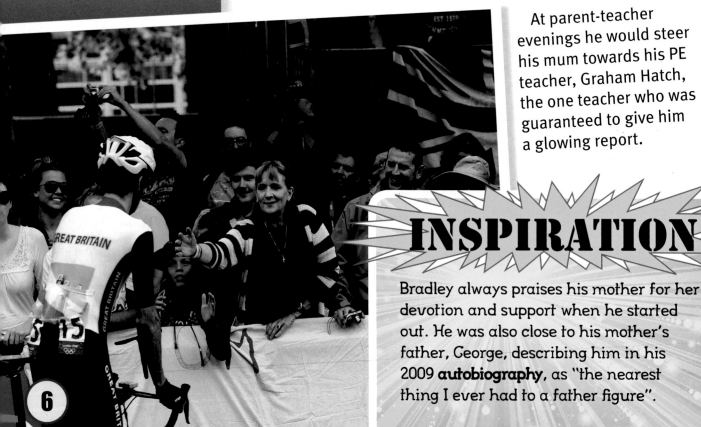

Bradley rides over to his mother, Linda, before the start of the 2012 Olympic road race.

Bradley and Linda moved back to London to live with Linda's parents, George and Maureen, later getting their own flat in Kilburn, London. Linda worked all hours to support her son and eventually became a secretary in the school Bradley attended – St Augustine's in Kilburn. Bradley liked school, although in interviews as an adult he has said that he wasn't a great student. He did enjoy sports such as football, cross-country running and baseball though.

At parent-teacher evenings he would steer his mum towards his PE teacher, Graham Hatch, the one teacher who was guaranteed to give him a glowing report.

INSPIRATION

Bradley always praises his mother for her devotion and support when he started out. He was also close to his mother's father, George, describing him in his 2009 **autobiography**, as "the nearest thing I ever had to a father figure".

Bradley was given his first bike when he was five. It was small, painted red and fitted with stabiliser wheels. Bradley couldn't wait to ride it, but not before he begged his mum to take the stabilisers off! Yet it was football that would prove to be his first sporting obsession. He started out as an Arsenal fan, but as most of his friends supported north London rivals Tottenham Hotspur (Spurs), he went to Spurs games to hang out with them.

As a football-mad kid, Bradley used to hide outside Gary Lineker's London house hoping to get a glimpse of the Tottenham and England striker. Bradley played football every day at and after school, and in the summer holidays took part in a six-week training camp at West Ham United where he played as a goalkeeper. He was playing football outside his home on July 29th, 1992 when his mother called him inside to watch something on television that would change his life.

WOW!

Bradley gained a stepbrother, Ryan, when he was seven, who now works as a teaching assistant at St Augustine's school alongside Bradley's old sports teacher, Mr Hatch.

TV presenter and former England footballer Gary Lineker runs with the Olympic torch. Live on television during the Olympics, Bradley was presented with a copy of a Royal Mail stamp celebrating his achievements by Lineker, his childhood hero.

Starting cycling

Bradley and Linda Wiggins sat down on their sofa on that day in July 1992 to watch the final of the 4km individual pursuit at the Barcelona Olympics. Linda remarked that this was an event Bradley's father had been really good at. Bradley was transfixed as Chris Boardman won Team GB's first cycling gold medal in 72 years and over the fortnight that followed watched plenty of other Olympic action as well. Bradley was inspired and told his mother that he wanted to win medals himself. In between watching the Olympics, he got on his bike and rode whenever he could.

Cycling in London wasn't easy with crowded roads so Bradley first cycled round the paths and trails of Hyde Park in London. He even cycled on an uncompleted road west of central London – the old Hayes Bypass – in a tatty old cycling helmet that had once been his father's.

TOP TIP

Bradley started paying attention to his diet at an early age, making sure he ate healthily to provide his body with enough fuel for the high energy demands of training and racing.

Chris Boardman powers round the Barcelona velodrome on his way to victory at the 1992 Olympics.

Before long Bradley was travelling across London to cycle at Herne Hill **velodrome** – which between 1987 and 2011 was the only cycle track in London. He also went on long training rides with a group of West London cycle enthusiasts who met up outside Acton train station. Bradley suffered his first serious cycling accident not long after when a car hit his bike and he broke his collarbone. It was painful and took a while to heal, but a **compensation** pay out the following year gave the family the funds to buy Bradley his first high-quality racing bike.

As Bradley progressed through his teens, he started to train harder, with his bike on rollers inside his family's flat when he couldn't cycle outside. He also became an avid reader of cycling newspapers and magazines. Success in his early races grew and grew until he became British Schoolboy Champion at the age of 15. Two years later, he was selected for the World Junior Championships in the South African city of Cape Town. Wiggins was on his way!

WOW!

After leaving school, Bradley became a trainee carpenter, working at the plush Lanesborough Hotel in London before starting a business studies course.

In this 2007 photo, Bradley stands with his childhood hero Chris Boardman, as they show their Olympic medals.

A first taste of glory

Bradley didn't win a medal at his first World Junior Championships, but at his second in 1997 in Havana, Cuba, he triumphed in the individual time trial, which for juniors is 3km long. The following year, in a major step up, he was selected for the GB adult cycling team competing at the **Commonwealth Games** in Kuala Lumpur, Malaysia. He narrowly missed out on a medal in the individual pursuit event there, coming fourth, but in the **team pursuit** won a silver medal – his first major medal in adult competition.

As a result of the win Bradley received his first major athlete funding from the National Lottery. It didn't make him wealthy, but it did give him the opportunity to concentrate on cycling and train even harder. He was now selected to train with the GB team at their base in Manchester. He worked as hard as he could to make it into the squad for the 2000 Olympics in Sydney, Australia.

WOW!

Bradley failed his driving test before the 2000 Games, so regularly had to take his bike by train from London to training sessions in Manchester.

Bradley (second on the right) celebrates with his bronze-medal-winning teammates in the team pursuit at the Sydney Olympics.

Bradley was incredibly excited to take part in the four-man team pursuit event at the Sydney Games. His team broke the British record for the 4km-long race with a lightning fast time of 4 minutes, 0.72 seconds, but were beaten by the team from Ukraine and had to be settle for bronze. Standing on the **podium** was an incredible thrill for Bradley.

On his return from Sydney, Bradley felt elated and excited, with his mind racing. His plans for pursuing a career in **professional** road racing were still there, but now he was also determined to add an Olympic gold to his bronze. It would take enormous amounts of hard work. Bradley launched himself into training and a demanding 2001 season, during which he took part in the World Championships in Antwerp, Belgium on the track and joined a professional team racing on the road in Europe.

INSPIRATION

Bradley had watched rowers Steve Redgrave and Matthew Pinsent on TV as a boy, and now he was inspired by meeting his heroes at the Olympic Village in Sydney. He wrote in his autobiography: "Their achievements will be proudly talked about in 100 years' time. That's an incredible sporting legacy to leave."

A broken wrist just a fortnight before the 2001 World Championships didn't stop Bradley from competing, and he won a silver medal in the team pursuit.

Highs and lows

Bradley's professional road racing career didn't start out well. The Linda McCartney Pro Cycling Team he joined for the 2001 season in Europe ran out of money quickly and he returned to Britain. The GB team welcomed him back and he got back into training and racing with them.

Bradley wears a streamlined helmet and skin-tight race clothing at the 2002 Commonwealth Games in Manchester.

The following year he joined another European pro team, *Française des Jeux*, but felt homesick and very much alone. When he was not selected by the team to take part in major races in the summer of 2002 this allowed him to return to Britain and take part in the 2002 Commonwealth Games, held in Manchester. Bradley won another silver medal in the team pursuit, but something even more significant was to happen at the Manchester Games.

WOW!

Bradley would become world champion six times between 2003 and 2012.

Bradley had first met Catherine Cockram back in 1997 when she was a promising sprint cyclist in the GB junior team. He liked her straight away, but didn't have the nerve to ask her out. At a party during the Commonwealth Games, they met again. Bradley and Catherine started going out soon after and were married two years later.

Bradley embraces his wife, Cath, and their two children, Ben and Isabella, after his victory in the 2012 Olympic time trial.

With Cath as his girlfriend, Bradley felt happy away from cycling, but needed a boost on his bike. Team GB felt he was underperforming and appointed Chris Boardman, who the 12-year-old Bradley had watched win Olympic gold, as Bradley's **mentor**. Boardman pushed him incredibly hard in training and questioned his attitude and professionalism at times. This approach worked and Bradley became a world champion for the first time, winning Britain's only gold medal of the 2003 World Championships in Stuttgart, Germany.

INSPIRATION

"Thank you Chris Boardman for being my initial cycling inspiration and then working so hard – with an occasionally difficult pupil! – to ensure I fulfilled my potential in 2004 and beyond" – Bradley Wiggins in his 2009 autobiography, *In Pursuit Of Glory*.

Olympic dreams

As the 2004 Olympics approached, Bradley felt in prime form. Team GB selected him for three different events at the Athens Games. Could his dream of Olympic gold come true?

Brad McGee and Bradley share a word after their close gold medal race at the 2004 Olympics. McGee had won the gold medal at the previous Games.

Bradley had been beaten a number of times in individual pursuit races by the great Australian rider, Brad McGee. After going through qualifying rounds and a tough semi-final, McGee was all that stood between the British cyclist and gold. After eight of the 16 laps of the 250m-long track, there was nothing in it, but in the second half of the race, Bradley **accelerated** and pulled away to win comfortably.

He was ecstatic and in tears as he cycled over to his wife, mother and stepbrother in the crowd. The next day, he was back in the saddle in the team pursuit, eventually winning a silver medal. He also teamed up with Rob Hayles to win bronze in the **Madison** event.

Returning home in triumph, Bradley was determined to relax and enjoy himself after all the hard work and sacrifices before the Olympics. He avoided serious training for months and on his return to road racing, was 7kg overweight and not giving his all. The birth of his son, Ben, jolted him back into action and with a strong 2007 season on the track gaining him two more world championship titles, Bradley looked set for success.

His preparations were rocked with the news in January 2008 of the death of his father in Australia at the age of 55. To this day, the mystery surrounding Garry Wiggins' death remains unsolved and Bradley struggled to come to terms with the terrible news. But with support from his family and friends and coaches within Team GB, he managed to focus for the Beijing Olympics.

At the 2008 Games Bradley scooped a further two gold medals, and was part of the winning team pursuit squad that smashed the world record twice during the event. He was disappointed, though, not to win a medal in the Madison with sprint great Mark Cavendish.

HONOURS BOARD

Bradley Wiggins' Olympic Medals

Sydney 2000
Bronze – team pursuit

Athens 2004
Gold – individual
  pursuit
Silver – team pursuit
Bronze – Madison
  (with Rob Hayles)

Beijing 2008
Gold – individual
  pursuit
Gold – team pursuit

London 2012
Gold – time trial

Bradley leads his GB team pursuit teammates around the bend of the Laoshan Velodrome on the way to winning gold at the 2008 Olympics in Beijing, China.

Taking on The Tour

As a teenager, Bradley's bedroom was covered in posters of cycling greats like Miguel Indurain and other winners of the *Tour de France*. He dreamt of racing in this epic event and in 2006 got his first chance as a junior member of the Cofidis race team.

TOP TIP

Bradley has learned that getting on with other members of a team or group you are a part of is vital to success. He learned to speak French so that he could communicate well with foreign riders.

The *Tour* is one of the most challenging endurance events in the world. Just under 200 of the world's most talented cyclists are timed as they race a tough 3,200km route divided into stages and held over three weeks. With only two days of rest out of 23, the *Tour* is one of the ultimate tests of cycling skill, **stamina** and as Bradley told GQ magazine in 2012, mental toughness. "For me, 80 per cent of the *Tour* is a mental challenge. Typically, you spend all year training towards it. You can't hold back...It is bigger, harder and more terrifying than any other event in cycling.

Bradley surges round a corner during the 2006 Tour de France. *His race team's sponsor was the French financial services company, Cofidis.*

WOW!

Bradley lost 7kg of weight in advance of the 2009 season to make it easier for him to make the tough climbs found in the *Tour de France.*

Bradley's first *Tour* was tough as he finished in 123rd place, but he was just relieved not to have been one of the 37 riders who failed to complete the race. He was amazed by how huge the *Tour* was, how there were hundreds of media people and thousands of fans at every location, and just how tough each day of racing was. On one **climb** through the Pyrenees mountains, Bradley lost five litres of sweat from his body in a just few hours and only narrowly managed to finish.

Bradley's 2007 *Tour* ended in controversy as his Cofidis team withdrew from the event (see page 23), and he did not compete in 2008. He did return to the *Tour* in 2009 with a different team, Garmin-Slipstream. Bradley had a great *Tour* and became only the second Briton since Robert Millar in 1984 to finish fourth in the *Tour de France.*

Part of a team

In 2009, a new British professional cycling team led by Dave Brailsford, the performance director of Team GB cycling, announced its aim to win the *Tour de France* within five years. Many cycling experts scoffed at such a target, but Team Sky were serious and quick to **recruit** some highly promising and talented riders including Edvald Boasson Hagen and Geraint Thomas. Bradley was installed as team leader.

Bradley's leading role meant that the other team members would ride for him, helping him to achieve as high a finishing position as possible in major road races. It placed plenty of pressure on Bradley to deliver strong performances but at the 2010 *Tour*, he could only manage a 24th place finish. For Team Sky, this wasn't good enough and the winter was spent boosting Bradley's training.

Bradley talks to Dave Brailsford during a winter training camp in Spain.

INSPIRATION

Dave Brailsford raced as a pro cyclist in France before taking university degrees in sports science and business. He has been a constant source of support for Bradley for over a decade. Bradley has described him as, "the best man manager I have ever encountered in sport".

It looked good for the 2011 season with Bradley winning a much-prized road race, the 1,064.4km-long *Critérium du Dauphiné* in June. He started the 2011 *Tour de France* well and was just 10 seconds behind the rider wearing the **yellow jersey** on the seventh stage when disaster struck. Involved in a nasty pile-up of 20 or so riders, he crashed to the ground and broke his collar bone, ending his participation in the race.

Bradley was philosophical after the race telling reporters, "It's unfortunate but life goes on and it's only bike racing, at the end of the day. When you have got 200 riders trying to stay at the front on small roads like that it's always going to happen. I've got fantastic form and it's only a broken collarbone. I'll recover from it and be back for the end of the season." And so it proved as he came third at the *Vuelta a España* as part of a strong Team Sky performance, with Chris Froome finishing in second place.

Bradley nurses his shoulder after crashing during the Le Mans to Chateauroux stage of the 2011 Tour de France.

WOW!

Just a month after breaking his collarbone in July 2011, Bradley was able to race to third place in the *Vuelta a España*.

A defining season

Bradley looked ahead to 2012 and knew it was going to be a huge challenge as the *Tour de France* and the Olympics in his home city were to be held within weeks of one another. He threw himself into intense winter training beforehand, knowing that if he suffered any setbacks or injuries he could probably not attempt both.

Fortunately, he emerged out of winter training in great condition and enjoyed a very successful start to the road racing season. An important test of form going into the *Tour de France* is the *Critérium du Dauphiné* event.

Team Sky dominated with three of the first four riders home, including Bradley, who won the race for the second time. He was now a real contender for *Tour de France* glory.

A large crowd lines the street to see the Tour riders streak past. Bradley is at the front wearing the famous maillot jaune (yellow jersey) which indicates the race leader.

Thousands of British cycling fans joined countless others in France lining all 21 stages of the famous race. Bradley started well, taking the yellow jersey as race leader after the 7th stage. With the support of his team members, he never lost the lead. He rode into Paris on the 22nd of July with a three minute, 21 second lead over teammate Chris Froome, who would finish second. After 3,496.9km of racing, Bradley Wiggins, had won the *Tour*. Sir Chris Hoy described the win as "the greatest individual achievement in the history of British sport".

In *The Guardian* newspaper the day after his triumph, Bradley explained how, "It's very difficult to sum up what I'm feeling in words. The thing that's struck me most over the last 12 hours or so is just what it means to other people around me, like my personal photographer breaking down in tears in my room, and my mechanic in tears as well; you just think hell, it's not just me who's gone through this, everyone else around me has lived it too."

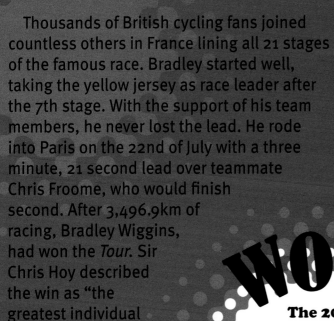

WOW!

The 2012 Tour de France was the first time in 99 years that two riders of the same nationality from the same team finished first and second.

Bradley on the podium as 2012 Tour de France winner, flanked by Chris Froome (left) and third place finisher, Vincenzo Nibali of Italy.

Le Gentleman

Bradley had been known to European cycling fans for a number of years, but in 2012 he earned praise and admiration not only for his victory but for his respect for the *Tour de France* and its traditions.

Bradley's keen sense of cycling history came from his childhood. According to British head coach, Shane Sutton, "When some kids ran to the park after school to play football, Bradley used to run home and put cycling videos on. He is an encyclopaedia of cycling."

Bradley speaks at a Team Sky press conference. As a top cyclist, he has to deal regularly with news and sports reporters.

WOW!

Bradley and Team Sky's bikes for the 2012 Tour were Pinarello Dogma 2 machines which weigh just 7kg but cost £10,000 each!

INSPIRATION

An improved mental attitude gave Bradley the belief he could win the Tour de France and for that he credits "the brain mechanic", sports psychologist, Steve Peters. Bradley calls him, "a professor in common sense" who helps Bradley banish nerves and doubts before big races.

During the 14th stage of the 2012 *Tour*, unknown saboteurs had sprinkled sharp tacks on the route which caused a number of riders to have punctures. One of those most affected was 2011 *Tour* winner, Australian cyclist Cadel Evans. As Evans suffered three punctures in a row and other riders were affected, Bradley, wearing the yellow jersey, insisted that the **peloton** slow down to allow Evans and others to rejoin the main group of riders. The French media began to call him, "Le Gentlemen" for this generous act.

Bradley has frequently spoken out against the use of doping – taking **performance-enhancing drugs** – in cycling and all sports. Bradley believes that doping is cheating pure and simple. He was a member of the Cofidis team who were thrown out of the 2007 *Tour de France* when one of their riders, Cristian Moreni, tested positive for a banned drug. Bradley was so disgusted at this cheating that on the way back home to Britain, he threw his Cofidis clothing and kit in a dustbin at Pau Airport.

Cadel Evans rides ahead of Bradley during the 2012 Tour. *Describing the Australian's 2011* Tour *victory, Bradley said "the way he won it inspired me to do it for myself."*

23

A day in the life of Bradley Wiggins

Most of Bradley's training days start with a healthy bowl of porridge or muesli, topped with seeds and fruits. Experts monitor his diet, fitness and health scientifically, and he has to watch what he eats at all times. It is not the only sacrifice. Long, **arduous** training camps and the huge demands of racing meaning that he can be away from home for weeks or months at a time. Bradley accepts it as part of being a top-flight cyclist.

Unless Bradley is recovering from a major injury, most of his work in the gym is performed to improve his core strength. Exercises involve working and strengthening the muscles of the back and body that cycling alone cannot easily improve. With greater **core strength**, Bradley is able to transfer more energy from his legs to his pedals, increasing his cycling power.

WOW!

When Bradley's in heavy training, he can burn up to 8,000 calories a day – that's three to four times the recommended daily intake for adults.

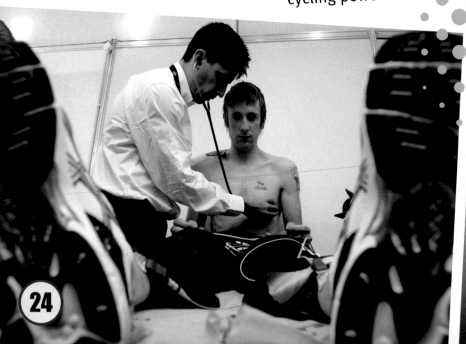

Bradley undergoes medical tests just before the 2007 Tour de France, *which began with a short stage through London before heading over to the continent.*

Most of Bradley's training, though, is on a bicycle. When asked where he was most at home by *Men's Health* magazine, Bradley replied, "Being in the saddle: it's my job. I ride a bike pretty much every day of the year, so it's become like a home." Bradley will often go on long 100-150km training rides with the rest of his team's riders or work on shorter, high-intensity climbs or sprints with one or more coaches for company. When not on the track or road, Bradley performs additional training at home with his bike on **static rollers**.

"Shane Sutton, our head coach, has a mantra – Train hard, race easy," Bradley told *The Telegraph* newspaper in 2012, and nowhere was that more seen than in the intense winter training ahead of Bradley's standout 2012 season. Some of it was brutal and involved a staggering 100,000 metres of steep hill climbs in warm conditions in the Canary Islands.

TOP TIP

Bradley believes that for you to achieve success you must devote yourself to your goals. In an interview with *Men's Health* magazine he said, "Put 100% into everything, even the little things. I put everything into even the smallest aspects of my training."

Training in the Spanish mountains, Bradley (second left at the front) rides with his fellow members of Team Sky. Getting on well together is an important part of a successful cycle racing team.

Away from competition

Competing, training and travel take up much of Bradley's time, but what does he do to unwind? Much of his spare time is spent with his family, from riding with his son, Ben, to taking the family to the cinema or on holiday.

Music is of great importance to Bradley. In a 2011 interview he said, "If I wasn't good at cycling I'd be just like any other person in London or Manchester who is into music and buying records." He had a large collection of vinyl albums usually stored in his shed in the garden of his home in Eccleston in Lancashire.

INSPIRATION

In an interview with *Cycle Sport* magazine, Bradley explained the effect music has on him. "Music to me is not just something you listen to. I've always been gripped by it … Music isn't a means of getting hyped up. It's a way of disconnecting from where I am."

It also houses his collection of more than a dozen guitars, one of which was owned previously by John Entwhistle, a member of the legendary rock band, The Who.

Ben Wiggins gets a guiding hand from his father as the pair cycle down the Champs-Elysées shortly after Bradley had won the Tour de France. Ben's bike is a scaled down replica of Bradley's.

Bradley retains an interest in football and follows Liverpool whilst he is also a season ticket holder at the DW Stadium in Wigan, where he watches rugby league side Wigan Warriors.

Despite his great success, Bradley does not see himself as a celebrity although he acknowledged in a 2012 *Daily Telegraph* interview that, "It's nice in sport when people stop you in the street and respect you for something you have achieved."

Bradley and his wife, Cath prefer seeing family and friends to going to lots of celebrity events, but exceptions are made, especially for music. A week after winning his London 2012 gold, Bradley and Cath, along with Jessica Ennis attended a secret gig in East London by The Stone Roses – along with the Smiths and Oasis, one of Bradley's favourite bands from Manchester. He also counts The Small Faces, The Jam and Paul Weller on his all-time playlist and was thrilled to receive a congratulatory Twitter message from Paul Weller straight after his Olympic victory.

WOW!

In 2012, Bradley's interest in mod fashion led to him designing a men's clothing range for the famous Fred Perry label.

Bradley poses for a photo with one of his musical heroes, Paul Weller, at an event in London in 2012.

The impact of Bradley Wiggins

Bradley Wiggins was an inspirational sportsman before his amazing 2012 season. Now, he is simply Britain's most successful cyclist ever. His generosity with spectators, down-to-earth manner and humour, and his racing prowess has earned him thousands of new fans. Wiggins has been a key part of Britain's highly successful Olympic cycling programme. Team GB has scooped an astonishing 18 gold medals in the last three Olympics and given cycling a massive boost as a leisure activity.

In the press conferences following his *Tour de France* and Olympic triumphs, Bradley highlighted the need for further laws to increase cycling safety, suggesting that cyclists need to help themselves stay safe and not wear music players while cycling.

TOP TIP

Bradley and other top cyclists including Sir Chris Hoy recommend that young cyclists always wear helmets and high visibility belts or jackets to help prevent serious injuries.

Bradley waves to other spectators inside the velodrome at the 2012 London Olympics as he watches the action alongside his son, Ben.

Early in 2012, Bradley set up an official charity – the Bradley Wiggins Foundation. Its aim is to get more young people into cycling and sport generally and to support talented young riders as they start out on a competition cycling career. His first major event for the Foundation, leading amateur cyclists on one of his typical training rides in Lancashire in August 2012, drew an incredible turnout of 2,000 cyclists, some coming from afar as Australia, Canada and the United States.

Bradley's career is far from over. If he stays fit, competitive and free of injury he can look forward to competing in further *Tours*, other road race competitions and even the next Olympics in Rio de Janeiro, Brazil in 2016. Further success will only increase the numbers of people he has inspired to take up cycling.

INSPIRATION

"He is a **role model**. It is fantastic what he has achieved. Cycling has been building for many years, but Wiggins is a lovely guy. He comes across as really genuine. He encourages his children to ride, and we hope that will encourage more parents to do the same." – Victoria Hazael of the Cycling Touring Club describing the 'Wiggins Effect'.

Children from Velo Club Londres cool down after a training ride around Herne Hill Velodrome, the cycling track where Bradley first raced as a 12-year-old boy.

Have you got what it takes to be a cycling champion?

1) Are you fit and do you enjoy sports that require lots of energy?
a) I love playing energetic sports and think I could be even fitter.
b) Occasionally, but I get tired out easily.
c) I'm not interested in getting that fit. I prefer watching sport to playing it.

2) How often do you choose to cycle?
a) Whenever I can and for as long as I can.
b) Sometimes, but only to visit my friends or to travel to the shops.
c) I only get on my bicycle in the summer holidays and then only once or twice.

3) How do you respond when you lose a race or sports match?
a) I'm gutted at the time, but think about how I can improve and win the next time.
b) Most of the time it doesn't bother me, but occasionally I get upset over losing.
c) I shrug my shoulders and get over it straight away. I don't think about it again.

4) Do you like being outdoors in all weathers running, cycling or playing outdoor sports?
a) I love it! Rain and cold rarely bother me.
b) I prefer to be outdoors only when it is warm and dry.
c) I much prefer being indoors with my computer and games machine.

5) How do you feel when you're faced with a steep hill to walk or ride your bike up?
a) I can't wait to tackle it. I love the challenge.
b) My heart sinks but I'll give it a go.
c) I'd avoid it if possible and choose a different route.

6) Are you prepared to sacrifice your social life to train for long hours?
a) Yes, that would not bother me.
b) I'm happy to do some training but I still want plenty of leisure time with my mates.
c) No chance. Going out with my friends is what matters to me.

RESULTS

Mostly As: It sounds like you have the right attitude, temperament and possibly the ability to enjoy competitive cycling. Why not find and visit your local cycle club? Many have welcome or open days where you can get a real feel for cycling as a sport.

Mostly Bs: It sounds like you enjoy some casual cycling, but nothing more than that yet. Why not challenge yourself with a longer ride with friends or family or visit a local cycle track to see some racing cyclists in action?

Mostly Cs: It doesn't sound as if you are cut out for a career in competition cycling – well, not yet anyway. But do try to hop on a bike when you can, not forgetting to wear a helmet. Cycling is great fun and good exercise, too!

Glossary

accelerate To increase speed.

arduous Hard work, requiring a lot of physical effort.

autobiography A book about a person's life written by that person.

climb Steep uphill parts of a road cycling course which really test a cyclist's strength and power.

Commonwealth Games A multi-sports event held once every four years and featuring athletes and competitors from around 70 different teams including England, Scotland, Wales, Australia and Canada.

compensation A sum of money paid out to someone who has suffered a loss or injury of some kind.

core strength The strength of the muscles in the human body's torso such as your shoulder, back or abdominal muscles (abs).

Madison A type of track cycling event featuring either two or three riders per team. At the Olympics until 2008, it was held over a distance of 50km.

mentor A trusted person who guides and advises another, providing them with support.

pacesetter In a time trial, the cyclist who is currently recording the fastest time.

peloton The main group of riders in a road race such as the *Tour de France*.

performance-enhancing drugs Substances taken to give an athlete an unfair advantage in their sport, such as enabling them to train for longer than usual or build muscles more quickly, and which may be harmful to their health.

podium The structure on which the first, second and third place competitors in an event stand to receive their medals.

professional A cyclist who is paid to be a member of a team and makes a living from competing in cycling competitions.

recruit To find and employ someone, such as inviting a cyclist to join a new racing team.

role model A successful person in sport or some other field. The way they behave is often copied by others, especially young people.

sponsors Companies who provide finance or equipment to a rider or a team.

stamina The ability to work hard for long periods of time.

static rollers A system of rollers on which a bicycle runs, allowing cyclists to ride their bikes and train without having to move from one place to another.

streamlined To be shaped so that the air moves quickly and smoothly over and past an object such as a cycling helmet.

team pursuit A type of track cycle race featuring four riders (or three riders in women's cycling) pursuing another team, trying to complete the distance in the fastest time.

time trial A race for individual riders against the clock where the winner is the fastest person to complete a set course.

velodrome A cycling track, usually oval in shape and 250-450m long, which can be outdoors or indoors.

yellow jersey Awarded to and worn by the race leader on each day of the *Tour de France*.

Index

Armstrong, Lance 17

Belgium 6, 11
Boardman, Chris 8, 9, 13
Boasson Hagen, Edvald 18
Brailsford, Dave 18

Cancellara, Fabian 5
Cavendish, Mark 4
Commonwealth Games 12, 13
Cuba 10
cycling safety 28

Ennis, Jessica 27
Entwhistle, John 26
Evans, Cadel 23

fans 4, 5, 21
Froome, Chris 5, 19, 21

Hatch, Graham 6, 7
Hayles, Rob 14
Herne Hill velodrome 9
Hoy, Sir Chris 21, 28

individual pursuit 14
Indurain, Miguel 16

Lineker, Gary 7

Madison 14
Martin, Tony 5
McGee, Brad 14
Millar, Robert 17
Moreni, Cristian 23

Olympic Games 4, 5, 7, 8, 10, 11, 14, 15, 20, 27, 28, 29
  Athens 14, 15
  Barcelona 8
  Beijing 15
  London 4, 5, 7, 15, 20, 27, 28
  Rio 29
  Sydney 10, 11, 15

pacesetter 5
performance-enhancing drugs 23
Peters, Steve 22
Pinsent, Matthew 11

Rand, Mary 14
Redgrave, Steve 11
road races 4, 19, 20, 29

South Africa 9
Sutton, Shane 22, 25

Team GB 5, 8, 12, 15, 18
team pursuit 11, 14
Team Sky 18, 19, 20, 22
Thomas, Geraint 18
time trials 4, 5
Tour de France 4, 16, 17, 20, 21, 22, 23, 28

Weller, Paul 27
Wiggins, Ben (son) 13, 15, 26

Wiggins, Bradley
  accidents 9, 19
  autobiography 6, 11, 13
  becomes world champion 13
  born 6
  British Schoolboy Champion 9
  charity 29
  designs clothing range 27
  diet 8, 24
  football fan 7, 27
  grandparents 6
  love of music 26, 27
  marries Catherine Cockram 13
  Olympic medals 5, 11, 14, 15, 27
  records 14, 15, 28
  school 6
  stepbrother 7, 14
  trainee carpenter 9
  training 8, 9, 10, 13, 20, 24, 25, 26
Wiggins, Catherine (wife) 13, 14, 27
Wiggins, Garry (father) 6, 8, 15
Wiggins, Isabella (daughter) 13
Wiggins, Linda (mother) 6, 7, 8, 14
World Championships 11, 13
World Junior Championships 9, 10

INSPIRATIONAL LIVES

Contents of new titles in the series

Amir Khan
978 0 7502 6809 7

World Champion!
A happy childhood
Bolton boy
Starting boxing
Amir the Olympian
A hero's return
Turning pro
Knocked down
Changing trainers
Success in the ring
A day in the life of Amir Khan
Charitable work
The impact of Amir Khan
Have you got what it takes
  to be a boxing champion?

Bradley Wiggins
978 0 7502 7737 2

Golden summer
Growing up
Starting cycling
A first taste of glory
Highs and lows
Olympic dreams
Taking on The Tour
Part of a team
A defining season
Le Gentleman
A day in the life of
  Bradley Wiggins
Away from competition
The impact of Bradley Wiggins
Have you got what it takes
  to be a cycling champion?

Steve Jobs
978 0 7502 6806 6

Daring to be different
The orphan who found a family
The founding of Apple
Steve leaves Apple
To infinity and beyond
A change of life
A day in the life of Steve Jobs
Gambling on the future
Putting music at your fingertips
Mission mobile
Running short of time
Reaching the end
The legacy lives on
Have you got what it takes
  to be the head of Apple?

Anthony Horowitz
978 0 7502 6808 0

A moment of inspiration
Anthony's family life
Off to Orley Farm prep school
A change for the better
Death in the family
A leap into children's writing
A day in the life of
  Anthony Horowitz
Anthony's big break
The Alex Rider series
TV, films and more books!
After Alex Rider
Helping charities
The impact of Anthony Horowitz
Have you got what it takes
  to be a writer?

Jay-Z
978 0 7502 6807 3

Jay-Z on top
Growing up in the projects
The wrong side of the law
A brush with death
Making history
Hitting the big time
Developing new artists
A day in the life of Jay-Z
Launching Rocawear
Selling the lifestyle
Crazy in love
Changing the game again
The impact of Jay-Z
Have you got what it takes to
  be a million dollar brand?

Usain Bolt
978 0 7502 6974 2

The world's fastest human
A lively child
Success comes early
Reality check
Time to rebuild
The world takes notice
Olympic superstar
Return of a hero
Lightning strikes twice
Awards and injuries
A day in the life of Usain Bolt
An inspiration to others
The impact of Usain Bolt
Have you got what it takes to
  be a record-breaking athlete?

WAYLAND